Yes! I AM

OPAL MURRAY

Yes! I Am
Opal Murray

Published by Pecan Tree Publishing
Hollywood, Florida

978-1-7358295-6-2 - Paperback
978-1-7358295-7-9 - Ebook
 Library of Congress Control Number: 2021902370

Cover Concept and Original Design by:
Rupa Limbu
Cover Design Revision and Interior Design by:
Jenette Antonio Sityar

Pecan Tree Publishing
www.pecantreebooks.com

New Voices | New Styles | New Vision
Creating a New Legacy of Dynamic Authors and Titles
Hollywood, FL

Acknowledgments

I offer thanks and praises to my Beloved Divine, ancestors, teachers, friends, and family. You have brought me to this place and time.

I extend heartfelt gratitude to Deborah Muise for telling me I could even as you faced your new realities.

Shelley Chapman, I am so blessed to walk in the light that manifests as your love and inspiration.

My heartfelt thanks to the many who supported me and cloaked me in excellence. Donna Zumstein, Eve, Frank Shulman, Janet A. Hastings, Jean, Molly A Lesnick, Molly St. Cavish, Nicole Shulman, Shayna N. Johnson, Shirley Edwards, Rev. Yvonne Graham, Violet Monica Wright-Grant, and you who chose not to be named.

Rev. Lori, Tanzua, Libzyyy, and Lori G. thank you for your generosity and willingness to share your knowledge.

Eckhart Teachings and Eckhart Tolle Now thanks for your permission to use the term 'pain-body'.

Pecan Tree Publishing how good and pleasant it is to have your guidance and talent. Thank you.

Finally, my sincerest thanks to you my dear Reader. I am honored that you have chosen to join me, so we bloom together and allow the fragrance of our I Am-ness saturate our communities with life-enhancing energy.

It is better to know yourself than someone to tell you who you are.

~ African Proverb

Table of Contents

Dear Reader:

Thank you for being here with me. Welcome to my second book, *Yes! I Am.* My first book was titled *I Am Precious: Nourishing Nuggets for the Heart; Genuine Gems for the Soul.*

It is quite likely that we have never met, yet I thought of you when I visited the San Jacinto Valley in California, in April 2019. Just about everyone I spoke with told me I had just missed the dazzling display of orange poppies. I saw the sparkle in their eyes and their spirited expressions of joy from being awestruck. I too got caught up in their stories and envisioned the breathtakingly beautiful landscape.

The locals gleefully shared the imagery of the California Poppy (the official state flower of California) in words and photographs. Their main story was centered around the "super bloom". Some say it had been at least five years since they witnessed this heartwarming, strikingly brilliant burst of orange/yellow blooms. Some did not like the hordes of visitors trampling on this soul-satiating spring extravaganza; but all attributed this exquisitely delightful explosion of flowers to the recent rains. As it turned out the area had suffered a multi-year drought. One long-time resident told me it had been so long since the flowers had bloomed, she had forgotten how visually stunning the poppies can be.

I share because as I heard story after story about how the rains helped the poppies to reveal their glory, I thought of you, Dear

Reader. You see, it occurred to me that this is the outcome I hope for Yes! I Am to achieve – I hope it stimulates your own stirrings for life. We encounter so many situations that can deny us our dignity, even our humanity. Bigotry, insensitivity, prejudgment, discrimination, any number of ideas or practices that say what you should do or who you should be. The truth, however, is that your life is waiting to be lived.

Mother Earth is nurturing over 7.5 billion of us humans. Every now and then someone tells me I resemble or remind them of someone they know. I am sure you have heard similar utterances. But even with our doppelgängers, we are still like the snowflake – unique, one of a kind! There may be physical or behavioral similarities, but you are the only one with the combination of names, parents, birthplace, education, possessions, friends, relatives, experiences, etc., that make you the person you are. Only you! How extraordinary is that!

It is only you who possess the agency, the desires, and the skills the way that you do. No one else! Only you can be you. You have this life to be just you, a spectacular you. Think about that and feel the profundity of this truth. The Greek philosopher and playwright, Euripides, reminded us that: "There is just one life for each of us – our own."

In California, poppies can cause such joy. Can you imagine if all these billions of us show our colors, our own beauty, our own agency, our own power? Perhaps it would create heaven here on earth.

In writing these pieces, I drew from a number of sources, some secular, some sacred. (Note: Even as I use the binary terms, I choose not to desecrate and therefore see all as sacred.) As an Interfaith student, I glimpse truth and divinity everywhere. I hope there is a morsel on these pages of *Yes! I Am,* that will help in revealing more of your own Self, just like the rain did for the California Poppy.

May you find nourishment in these quotations, 28 musings, and the trinity of poems to spark your somebody-ness, unearth your uniqueness, embolden your agency, delight in your Self, or hearten your urge to answer to the calling of your authentic Self – your life.

Again, thank you for sharing this space with me. I am honored. Let's shout it to the universe, but more so to our Self, *Yes! I Am.* Be delightfully delighted.

Yes! I Am!

I Am
So many parts

I Am
Connected with all things

I Am
Me

I Am
Beloved and divine

I Am
Secular and earthy

I Am
As vast as the universe

I Am
Confined to the prism of now

I Am
Here and in a twinkle

I Am
There

I Am
Magic

I Am
Love

I Am
All and yes, One

I Am
Me

May my orgasmic shout
Be recorded in paradise

Yes!
I Am!

Those who know others are intelligent.
Those who know themselves are truly wise.
Those who master others are strong.
Those who master themselves have true power.

-Tao Te Ching
translated by J H McDonald

Holy Self

I Am Holy

In my youth, I was fascinated by my initials – OOM. As I became a student of the customs humans use to experience the Divine, I was in awe when I found out that when my initials are pronounced, they give the sound – 'ohm', the sacred sound of our Hindu family. I also found it is an honored mantra of Buddhists, Jains, and Sikhs.

OM is the disambiguation of AUM, the components of the three stages of the cosmic creation. AUM celebrates the creative powers of the universe. Basically, 'Ah', coming out of the throat is the beginning. 'Uu' comes inside the mouth representing fullness and 'Mm' buzzes as the lips close returning the sound to the throat signifying completion. One gets the same sense by observing the lunar cycle – the waxing moon, then it becomes full and then it wanes.

This sacred trinity is represented in many forms when honoring the Holy. The universal sound has become more personal, in that I find it to be true for all beings, all existence – an entrance, a fullness, a departure.

May we bathe in holiness as we chant AUM.

Yes! I Am holy.

Evolving

I Am Unfolding

We learn about Kundalini Awakening from our Hindu family. It is the movement of our life force energy up the spinal column flowing through each chakra.

It is believed that we have seven chakras or seven spiritual centers connecting our mind, body, and soul. The first four are the root, sacral, solar plexus, and heart chakras. The root chakra governs our basic needs – food and other material possessions. When we live at the level of our sacral chakra, we become more concerned about sexual pleasure and procreation. Some of us graduate to the third level – the solar plexus, the region of the upper abdomen. Here we become confident in ourselves living with our well-fed egos. Many of us find these three areas to be the ultimate in living. At this level, we have the material and physical necessities of life. We are satisfied. This space could make us arrogant or confident and perhaps even self-centered. We begin to trust in our "chariots and horses" forgetting that the Hebrew psalmist (Psalms 20:7) cautioned us not to place much hope in technological or material riches. But it is so easy to get comfortable and be lulled into remaining at this level of our development.

Fortunately, we have had teachers who show us we can evolve. These leaders continued to grow and had the courage to open to the awakening at the heart level. They were born again, learned to love unconditionally, and how to become deeply compassionate. In this space, they experienced inner peace.

Others who continued on the path opened themselves to the remaining three levels: throat, third eye, and crown chakras. Living at the fifth level - throat - there is freedom to express our inner truth. The truth which was learned at the heart level. As we enjoy the freedom of expressing and living our truth, we are now ready to experience the sixth chakra or third eye, where we learn more about universal mysteries and powerful discernment skills. In the Gnostic Bible, *The Pistis Sophia*, we learn that after Jesus had risen from the dead, he spent eleven years instructing his disciples. In one of the sessions (Book One Chapter 24), Mary Magdalene apologized to her Lord for frequently asking "troubling questions." Jesus encouraged her to ask nevertheless, telling her he "will reveal it to thee in all openness." I imagine the disciples had reached the third eye in their consciousness and the way to the universal oneness, the crown chakra, was being revealed.

It was Mark Twain who said: *"The two most important days in our life are the day you are born and the day you find out why."*

May we be elevated from the trappings of our basic lower chakras. May we have the wisdom and courage to open our Selves to the wealth of our entire humanity.

Yes! I Am unfolding to reveal the wealth of my humanity.

Self-Healing

I Am Healing

Some of us believe that if we are wronged, our only recourse is to harm another. Some say that is justice. But justice is in the hands and heart of the one who dispenses it. The social justice advocate will argue a different point from the retributive justice proponent. The former will ask for fairness and will consider the value of humanity while the latter clings to thoughts of crime and punishment.

What is troubling is that we find both examples of social and retributive justice recorded in the Christian Bible. There are the teachings of Jesus, most notable when he negated the Mosaic law of "taking a life for a life; eye for an eye; tooth for a tooth; hand for hand; foot for a foot; burn for burn; wound for wound; bruise for bruise." Jesus instead taught that if "anyone slaps you on your right cheek turn to them the other cheek" (Matthew 5: 39).

On the other hand, the story in Genesis 34 gives us a lot to consider in determining the benefits of retributive justice. The story is about Jacob's daughter, Dinah. Dinah was in an intimate relationship with Shechem, who was Prince Hamor's son. (The stories range from them being in love to Shechem raping Dinah.) When her brothers, especially Levi and Simeon, heard about the relationship they were angered. Shechem and Dinah loved each other and wanted to marry. Shechem asked his father to negotiate the marriage with Jacob. Dinah's brothers said the family would only agree if Shechem and all the men agreed to be circumcised. Shechem was happy that he would marry his love. He agreed to the conditions, he and the men of his father's land would be circumcised. We learn that on the third day after the procedure, when Shechem and his tribesmen were sore and in pain, Levi and Simeon pounced on their infirmed state and massacred Shechem and his compatriots to avenge their sister's honor.

Some attitudes today seem to align more with the Mosaic position than with Jesus' teachings. It was Dr. Martin Luther King, Jr. who cautioned us when he said, "If we do an eye for an eye and a tooth for a tooth, we will be a blind and toothless nation." Is this the vision we have for future generations?

May we open our hearts to justice that is infused with compassion knowing that forgiveness not only heals the offender but our selves as well.

Yes! I Am healing My Self and the Other Selves.

Life United Part 1

I Am This and That

It is a funny thing – this brain of ours. It is one organ with two distinct sides possessing billions of nerve cells performing billions of functions. Scientists say it is the most complex object in the universe. To help us grasp these complexities, they filtered the functions into two areas to explain how the brain impacts our behavior using the binary right and left.

Based on earlier studies, many people still subscribe to the notion that we are dominated by either the left or right side of our brain. That we are either creative or analytical. Modern research by the University of Utah Health Services has debunked this theory and scientists now say there is a collaborative and cooperative working relationship with both sides of the brain. For instance, while the left side can identify the sounds that form words, it is the right that detects the expressive meaning – joy, sadness, etc.

Jill Bolte Taylor, PhD., neuroanatomist and author, suffered a stroke, and as she recalls, the left parietal region of her brain went offline. When that happened, she tells us, the consciousness of her right brain did not recognize the boundaries of her body. She said she felt as big as the universe. Her spirit soared free. She reminds us that our ancient ancestors lived mainly from the right brain. They lived in the present moment and their primary concerns were food, shelter, and mating. They lived in community and looked out for each other.

In our recent history, the shift has been to live more left-brained. We have become more material-oriented; mine and yours. We have succumbed to our desire to have more. For me, I want more travel. (Machu Picchu, I have you in my sights!) When we believe that resources are limited, we compete to the point where we become willing to maim and murder our fellow beings to acquire those resources.

What is curious about Dr. Taylor's view on life, having experienced the thrill of her soaring spirit and the expansiveness she felt when her left brain was damaged, is she realized that for life to exceed the mundane she had to have the binary condition of the left and the right. It is important to operate from both areas of our brain, she tells us. Sometimes we need to come together in community and other times our individuality must be nourished. When we experience an up, we should be comfortable with the down, our happy will find our sad. Whatever it is that we face, it is temporary. It has come to pass - not in the sense of a revelation but to keep moving, it is transient. Competition and cooperation are part of our DNA. We are not to harm others when we compete, and we shouldn't harm ourselves when we cooperate.

Zen Master, Thích Nhất Hạnh, teaches us: "Our suffering is impermanent and that is why we can transform it; and because happiness is impermanent that is why we have to nourish it."

May I consciously experience my This and my That.
May my This comfort my That and may my That protect my This.
May I understand my This and That reflect my unified Divinity.

Yes! I Am my This and my That.

Success-Self

I Am Success

Almost daily I receive electronic inspirational messages. One such message was an acrostic on success, but it didn't feel right to me. What it did though was to inspire me to dig deeper in my rabbit hole and create a vision of success that felt truer.

Success
S – See myself
U - Understand who I am
C - Take time to Contemplate
C – Have the Courage to master self
E – Excel in what I love to do
S – Speak kindly and with integrity
S – Smile with myself and others

S – *See myself.* The ancient Greeks inscribed the words "Know thyself" on a wall in the Temple of Apollo at Delphi. Self-knowing or self-awareness is the foundation of our existence.

Legendary reggae artist, Bob Marley, encourages us to "open our eyes and look within."

U – *Understand who I am.* Greek philosopher, Socrates told us "an unexamined life is not worth living." I must take the time to understand who I am, my skills, my desires, my ancestors, my quirks, my blood pressure numbers, my feelings, the people, and events that have impacted my life. This knowing will give me shelter in the storms of life and wings when it is time to rise.

C – *Take time to Contemplate.* Even Jesus would often take time to be away from it all. I too must seek my quiet place to commune with what is greater than I am.

C – *Have the Courage to Master Self.* (This is why U is so important.) Our society is filled with so many of us who ignore our affairs to tell others how they ought to act, feel, who to love, what to buy, where to worship, etc. Sometimes we find that we are that obnoxious person. Sometimes we are convinced and feel that we have the necessary insights but many times it is only a distraction to keep us from looking inward. To succeed I must have courage, the courage to be true to myself.

E – *Excel in what I love to do.* Yes, we can excel by sheer determination and being strong-willed, but we can also excel by loving. When we love what we do, to the onlooker, success is fun and appears easy because we show no signs of stress or anxiety.

S – *Speak kindly and with integrity.* As a child, one of the first lessons I learned from the Christian Bible is the Hebrew proverb – A soft answer turns away wrath. I don't always succeed but when I do, I realize that I gave life and love to the receiver and I walk away feeling lighter.

S – *Smile with myself and others.* Psychologists say that babies learn as early as five weeks old, that while it is crying that gets the adults' attention, it is by smiling that they keep the adults' attention. A Mongolian proverb says, "A heartfelt smile gives warmth enough for three winters." As a two-month-old, we knew this, but we have forgotten. Smiling allows us to connect with others – which is a big part of our existence: to be in community, to connect.

Success starts when we see ourselves. It is only true when there is community. Success is not a solo flight. It touches all it meets.

May my success give light to others so that they may know what is possible.

Yes! I Am the light from my success.

Determined Self

I am Rising Even ...

If we are lucky, we would have had a front seat to witness the marvel of toddlers attempting to walk. You will notice that they stand, or pull themselves up, wobble a bit, and fall. Without coaxing, they make another attempt. Then over time, it happens. They take that miraculous first step.

For those of us who were ambulatory as toddlers, we have done that. Between that first step and when we die, so many adventures and experiences are lived. There are a few of us who will live in a milieu of love, encouragement, approval, and goodwill. Some of us will meet the horrors of abuse or neglect. Many of us, though, will live in a world that offers a pinch of the former and a dash of the latter.

While navigating this world, we concentrate on the present joy or pain. We start to live in this environment with its externally-induced situations. As we move into adulthood, the truth of our inner strength, our inner knowing becomes dim. We no longer draw on that knowledge that served us when, as toddlers, we had the impulse to walk. Even as we fell, we knew we should get up. We fell, we got up. Repeat. Then voila! We walked.

This basic experience has a parallel. It's our formal education/ school system. Unfortunately, in this system falling or failing has dire consequences. Others tell us we are a failure when that happens. This causes that primordial instinct – the inborn knowing - to get snuffed out of us. There will be times when we become aware of an internal, divine spark. We may attempt to grasp it but just as our first attempt to walk, we are likely to miss the mark.

Some of us will just accept the outcome because we are convinced by our environment that we can't. Some will make another attempt, but one can only keep trying for so long. So, if the desired result hasn't manifested itself then we tend to move on to something more expedient. The wisdom of the toddler has been tucked away and exchanged for educated knowledge. However, a few of us will remember, and we will continue the journey falling and getting up until, like our toddler self, the goal is achieved.

Many books are written about determination and success but if we can recall experiencing the miracle of a child attempting to walk, then we will have the entire story. Remember, children begin to walk in their own time. Our success is not to be compared to the success of others, no matter the similarities. It happens in its own time at the right time.

Remember when you took that first step? After all that effort, it was the beginning of something new as is the case when we succeed. Determination opens doors for us to take even more steps. Like nature our lives have cycles. Perhaps it is winter, being held; spring, a crawl; summer, the walk; and autumn, the run. As adults, we are held and supported by our dreams and our communities. We crawl by understanding our dreams – researching, learning, being mentored, etc. We implement our dreams each time we experience what appears to be a setback, we learn and strengthen our resolve. We take some time off to evaluate, then return to the truth of our dream.

May we be determined to succeed even when all we see are stumbling blocks.

Yes! I Am remembering how to get up after falling.

Self-Care

I Am Nourishing My Self

I was so concerned that Other Selves would see me as selfish. So much so I buried, drowned, cast aside, locked away, or just ignored any thought of paying attention to my Self. No, no. I did not want to be labeled selfish. Or worse, seen as vain to my physical self.

But that was then.

It was while facilitating a training session for volunteers on the importance of self-care in accomplishing the task for which they had enlisted when I actually heard myself speak. The activities I categorized as vain and selfish should have been considered self-care. Futurist Alvin Toffler said, "The illiterate of the 21st century will not be those who cannot read and write, but those who cannot learn, unlearn, and relearn." Rather than remaining illiterate, I decided to rewind and relearn.

To be selfish is having concern only for your Self while ignoring all others. Self-care on the other hand is a practice that encompasses my physical, emotional, financial, psychological, and spiritual well-being. It is not only desired; it is necessary if I am to be healthy. To practice Self-care, it is critical for me to nurture every aspect of my being.

By no means am I comparing myself to the saints, but I connected with one of the greatest thinkers in antiquity - the African Catholic, Saint Augustine. I learned that he too struggled with his physical self to the point where he begged his God to rid him of his strong desires for sex, food, and alcohol. St. Augustine was well acquainted with his physical Self and he knew that his desires were incompatible with his vows; so, he sought help.

Another saintly figure, Siddhartha Gautama, chose not to struggle with the aspect of his Self that wanted to be freed. To care for his spiritual Self, he deserted his life of privilege and answered the call to feed the spiritual aspect of his being. His willingness to surrender to this need led him to Buddhahood.

Self-care is related to being self-aware. Because it is by being self-aware, we learn what our Selves are seeking. When we read the biography of the people we admire, we feel the thirsts and curiosity that drove them. We learn how they remained true to that part of them that required attention. We learn how they turned away from what they found injurious and faced what made them leaders. St. Augustine gave us permission to face the truth of our physical Self. The Buddha showed us how to quench the thirst of our spiritual Self.

Self-care is not to be a transitory catchword. Instead, it should be etched in our lived experiences. It is an opportunity for us to be true to our Selves, to be self-aware, to adopt the ancient command "Know thy Self" as our mantra. It is the practice that frees us to love our Selves, see our wholeness, and gives us the peace from our God that passes all understanding. It helps us to be comfortable in our skin – the entire package. It guides us to care for our Selves.

May we see our Selves as a total entity.
May we cherish and care for each of our Selves.

Yes! I Am nourishing all of my magnificent Self.

Self- Exploration

I Am Curious

The Shape of Water has been described as an adult fairy tale movie. It has had its controversies e.g.; plagiarism and the idea of a mute person being attracted to a monster. However, I find that the movie gave us an opportunity to reexamine our image of God; to consider how we communicate with each other; to be convinced of what we know is true for us. It also gives the opportunity for us to explore who will show up as members of our community when we need help.

Let's have a look at each of these ponderings.

#1 – What is your image of God?

In some faiths, there are no images of a God. For others, it's prohibited. In some, artists are free to project their thoughts and create a God based on their likeness. In others, there are multiple representations of the Gods and Goddesses. In the movie, one character settled the argument by thinking out loud his supremacy, musing that he probably looked more like God than the female who was present. He also found it ridiculous that an amphibian creature could be a God as his worshippers claimed it to be.

Have you ever wondered what your God or Goddess looks like? Are you an image of that God or Goddess? If not, do you know why not? How does your answer impact your view of your Self and your world?

#2 – How do you communicate with your Self and your Others?

The movie showed us that it was the mute woman who communicated with Amphibian Man. She used signs. Having been mistreated and abused by other humans through words, Amphibian Man needed more than words to enter dialogue with her. So, signs of tenderness and compassion became the vehicles for communication. There was respect, a sense of equality, and perhaps the gifting of eggs. This gifting seems to mirror a favorite story of the over two billion Christians worldwide – the Wise Men bringing gifts to baby Jesus.

As you sit with your memories of how you communicate with Others, ask: Am I being kind? Am I respectful? Am I seeing my Other as an equal being?

I've heard it said "Before we speak, we should answer 'Yes' to three critical questions – Is it true? Is it necessary? Is it kind?" Also, never underestimate the power of meaningful gifts – gifts given without conditions from a grateful, open-heart; gifts imbued with love.

#3 – What do you know to be true?

This can be very difficult because a) situations change and b) there can be so many voices sharing their truth or their understanding. One of the more than one hundred ancient Delphic sayings 'Know Your Self' is still true today. Take the time to check in with your Self daily; honor your skills; feel what animates your Being; seek what is healthy for You; align with your dreams. When you know what you know to be true, magic follows.

The mute woman knew she had to free Amphibian Man. When this flooded her being as the right action, known and surprising allies showed up to help her accomplish her task.

#4 – Who will you call?

Continuing with movies. The original *Ghostbusters* movie popularized the phrase "Who you gonna call?" Ask your Self who would you call when the world is closing in on you? Who is there for you to laugh with, to cry with you, to say no to you, to say yes to you, to celebrate with you, to mourn with you? Who are the members of your community who will not judge you, who will be there for you?

It is time for us to appreciate the power of interdependence. Our lives are woven together. This shift in belief will help to harmonize our living. In the Hebrew tradition, we hear a lot about Moses and less about Aaron and Hur. But as the story goes, had it not been for them holding up Moses' arms, the Israelites would have lost the

battle (Exodus 17). We need our community as we travel this life –
in both victory and defeat.

*May we be blessed with light and truth as we query
our life and beliefs.*

Yes! I Am mining my soul.

My Body, My Home

I Am at Home in My Body

Teasing, bullying, and shaming are experiences felt on many playgrounds. I remember as a child, growing up in Jamaica – a place where, it seems, every sound, smell, and sighting pleased the senses, I was made to feel that I was not pretty enough to be a member of this exquisite landscape. The verdict was made on the playground. My nose was too flat.

These days we hear or read about "body shaming" or "body positive" stories in the public squares. We have individuals who make it their duty to mock the bodies of other humans because the bodies they mocked fail to demonstrate the perfection that the mockers imagine. Such derision, however, has repercussions. There are stories of aspiring entertainers not being engaged because s/he didn't have the arbitrary unstated requirement of what is deemed beautiful.

Body positive proponents encourage us to love and respect our bodies. This can be a hard sell. Whether or not we agree with the terms, we operate in a world where the material, the things seen, take preeminence over unseen qualities. Rev. Dr. Martin Luther King, Jr's. dream of people being judged by "the content of their character rather than the color of their skin" was offered as an alternative way of gauging who our Others are.

The Apostle Paul guided his converts in Philippi in what to consider when making an assessment "...whatever is true, whatever is pure, whatever is lovely, whatever is admirable, if anything is excellent or praiseworthy, think about these things." (Philippians 4:8)

How about using this list, in this moment, to admire and honor our bodies? The vessel that houses our mind, heart, soul, and all the organs that work together so the body can show up. Consider its truth, nobility, rightness, purity, and loveliness. Right now, let us praise the entire miraculous package.

The exercise of praising our bodies may awaken a deeply painful experience that the body is holding on to. While therapy may offer healing, at times massaging, speaking love to the area, or listening and responding to our body may provide some relief for these hurts. Lifting the pain could hasten our arrival to the heavenly spot where we claim what is ours with no shame. We become more hopeful that it is possible to get to the point in our journey where we are freed to dance, to celebrate the uniqueness of our flat noses and all the elements that conspired with each other while traveling six million years to create the human being we see in the mirror. Isn't that awesome?

May we be wise and claim the body that is ours.

Yes! I Am at home in my body.

I Am the Greatest!

I Am my GOAT

Goat is no longer just an animal. It is now accepted that GOAT also means *Greatest of All Times.* This title is lauded on individuals who excel in their field. Many times, an athlete is described as a GOAT i.e., boxer Muhammad Ali.

Many of us admire his skills as a boxer as well as how he showed up as a human being. If asked, I am sure you have your own list of GOATs. I believe it is also true you will not have your name on that list. You do not see yourself as a GOAT. But it is true, each of us possesses all that is needed to be our own GOAT. We were created to be the greatest us ever! There is no one like you, with your talents, your desires, your path. No one! Only you.

In his 1931 publication, *Heal Thyself,* English doctor, homeopath, and spiritual writer, Edward Bach wrote that when "...our souls and personalities are in harmony, all is joy and peace, happiness and health." Isn't this what we see – a harmonizing essence – projecting from our GOATs? Yet as enticing as this is, we withhold the experience from our Selves.

In the First Book of Samuel in the Christian Bible, there is the well-known story of David and Goliath.

Reading the story as an adult, I am struck by a particular series of events and decisions David made. When the king and his council agreed that David would meet Goliath, after laughing at David because they said he was young and inexperienced in battle, David was suited in the king's armor: a helmet of bronze; a coat of metals, and a sword. This was first-class war technology! David was not impressed by this arsenal. He was not in harmony with his environment. He told the king, "I cannot go with these; for I am not used to them." (1 Samuel 17: 39).

David undressed from these technologically-advanced devices and went to Goliath with what he was used to. Tools that are quite ordinary: a sling, five smooth stones from a brook, his shepherd's bag, and a staff.

Having spent time in the fields, David, I imagine, had time to contemplate and better understand who he was – his skills and areas of expertise. Having fought with lions and bears to protect his sheep, he was confident in his abilities. He knew his truth.

Unfortunately for humanity, our education system is geared to help us get a job just as the king wanted to educate David so he could have a job. Every now and then we see a modern David who escapes and follows what is the core of her/his being – Paulo Coelho, Maya Angelou, Steve Jobs, Frida Kahlo, Oprah Winfrey.

I do understand there are bills to be paid. Shelter, food, clothing, and even entertainment are needed, and they come at a financial cost. Because of these constraints, we feel we cannot take off the armor placed on us by others and instead use what we know to be true about ourselves. For some of us, we did not have the opportunity to contemplate two fundamental questions: Who am I? and What are my skills, dreams, and desires? Yet, because we have not considered them, that doesn't mean they do not exist. I believe the answers are waiting to be uncovered.

In his book *Heal Thyself,* Dr. Bach taught that there are two errors humans make. One, showing up in life contrary to the dictates of our souls: "dissociation between our souls and personalities." The second, causing "cruelty or wrong to others." When we become our own GOAT, we correct both errors. The harmonizing essence we experience, like that of our cherished GOATs, gives us peace and joy. This sense of happiness and contentment reduce the need for us to direct hostilities toward others and guide us to the field of oneness. Or as Dr. Bach prefers, we act in unity.

May we be the GOAT we admire.

Yes! I Am a GOAT. I will be the greatest me.

Self-Evolution

I Am finding my Bedrock

At a recent session on *The Spirituality Found in Dr. Seuss' Writings*, we read and discussed his book *The Zax*. The story is about a North-Going Zax and a South-Going Zax who met at the same point in their journey. They stubbornly refused to yield so the other could pass and allow both to continue with their northerly and southerly journey. After some bickering, North-Going Zax said: "I have never taken a step to one side and I'll prove to you that I won't change my ways if I have to keep standing here 59 days." Not to be outdone, South-Going Zax vowed to stand in his spot for 59 years because he learned in school to never budge. So, there they stood, not budging, through day and night, rain, and sunshine, winter, and summer. Meanwhile, their world didn't standstill. Their world changed around them and left them encased in their stubborn belief not to budge.

I agreed with the premise that as humans, living organisms, we are meant to grow, develop, evolve, and change.

I also believe we must not be like a dry leaf and get tossed here and there by the winds of other people's ideas or by circumstances. But wait, what about the evolving bit? What if I experience something new and it sparks a truth that was entombed inside me? Should I not explore this new awakening and perhaps even embrace its unfolding and as a result become a changed person?

In one of Jesus's teachings, he likened humans to a builder who builds his house after he had dug deep to lay its foundation on the bedrock. In this way, the outer circumstances such as floods, will not destroy the house. Unlike another where its builder placed the house on a hollow, unreliable foundation making the house susceptible to damages from external influences.

We are these houses the great Way Show-er spoke of. There is our innate truth which is our core. Think of the artists, athletes, scientists, writers, etc. we admire. Think about how they showed up and demonstrated their skills. They drew from what is true about them. They accepted the training. Maybe they went through untold difficulties, having to overcome naysayers or bullies who ridiculed them.

They may have faced setbacks brought on by financial or relationship woes. Whatever the difficulties were, they kept going. They kept drilling. They kept changing, always moving to their truth, to the beat of their own drum. Always facing their North Star. They changed. They grew. They developed new strategies. They used new tools and always or at least most times, moving inward, drilling deeper to find that bedrock within them. Changing so that they can get to their Promised Land.

I am still drilling into my bedrock. I hear, though, that when we get there, we will find a sense of peace and we will shine brightly. Alex Haley had not reached his bedrock. He was rejected 200 times by publishers who did not value his epic novel, Roots. Instead of giving up, he drilled deeper. Eventually, his ground-breaking work exposing historical events, previously hidden, was published. It later became a record-smashing television miniseries.

We should never allow our lives to be aimless. But when we feel we're being tossed; it may be useful to look at each circumstance and learn why it has presented itself. Chances are it came to share knowledge or understanding or wisdom. It could be there to guide us to dig deeper. Pema Chödrön, Tibetan Buddhist nun, says: "Nothing ever goes away until it has taught us what we need to know."

Perhaps you have built the best and strongest house and you are firm in your bedrock. You have excelled and your entombed truth is freed to bless our world. Have a moment with this mountaintop experience. Close your eyes. When you are ready, open them. Like Nelson Mandela, you will not only see "the glorious vista that surrounds you, but you will see there are many more hills to climb."

Even while anchored in the loving embrace of our innermost self, change can beckon us to keep moving. Keep being used up. Keep being more. Not in an egocentric way but in a manner that shows benevolence and fullness. We see the extension of our journey, our more hills. We get propelled by a generosity of spirit to keep going. We grow. We advance, all the while facing our North Star. We evolve knowing our Truth beckons.

May we keep moving to our Truth.

Yes! I Am evolving. Yes! I Am finding my Bedrock.

Hopeful Living

I Am Hoping

In Greek mythology, there are three stories about Pandora's Box. One story tells us that the gods gave Pandora a sealed jar, which was a gift to humanity. After some time, Pandora's curiosity overpowered her, and she opened the jar. Well, out flew disease, pain, envy, suffering, death – all the dreadful things that would bring misery to mankind. A surprised and sorrowful Pandora realized what had happened, hurriedly closed the jar trapping the only item left – hope.

A second story tells of her husband, Epimetheus, having the world's misfortunes sealed in a box in his house. Again, we see Pandora's curiosity leading her to open the box. Again, out flew this group of ills. When she sensed what was happening, she closed the lid but again, hope was captured inside the sealed box.

The third story tells us that Zeus had sent a box of blessings as a wedding present. Pandora carelessly opened the gift and the blessings escaped and returned to the heavens. Again, she realized what was happening. She quickly closed the lid, but hope was slow and was locked in the box.

Whichever version you believe, the Greeks learned that humanity had only hope to help them deal with the evils, tragedies, and pains that we face in life.

Jesus told his followers that even if they had faith as small as a mustard seed, they would move mountains, and overcome any challenge. Jewish teachings say the greatest commandment is love. The Greeks spoke of hope. Years later, the Christian Apostle, Paul, who I believe was familiar with Greek mythology, as well as Jesus' teachings and Jewish doctrine, collapsed the three tools of survival he gleaned from these belief systems. Paul told us we have this trifecta of tools to guide us into living well-intentioned and meaningful lives. He went on to point out that love supersedes the other two. (I'm not sure if he created a true hierarchy or gave faith and hope equal billing behind love.)

Seldom do we hear of faith or hope outside the religious or spiritual arenas. Love on the other hand is spoken of everywhere. In popular culture it is pervasive. Many forms of art present love as a physical action, psychologists speak of multiple forms of love. Some belief systems, like Sufism - Islamic mysticism - see love as the reason we exist. Love runs the gamut of the physical flesh to esoteric teaching. Faith and hope are usually linked to pipe dreams - wishing and hoping.

But what if we were to take time for quiet introspection and open our jar of hope? Examine our hope. What is it that we hope for our life, this life we now have?

I believe that in our hope we will be guided to loving it and believing in its reality. So much so, that we will move it from its dream state and make it real. Remember, even the chair you're sitting on was once someone's dream. Someone's hope.

May we hope for what is true for us.

Yes! I am the hope I dream of.

Guided Living

I Am Letting Go

Both the Hebrew Scriptures (Genesis 19) and the Quran (26: 161-173) introduce us to a man named Lot (In the Quran it is Lut). We are told that angels warned him to take his family and flee because the city in which they lived would be destroyed. The Genesis story goes on to say that as the family left "...Lot's wife looked back and was turned into a pillar of salt." The Quran is less graphic and teaches us that Lut and his family were delivered except for an "old woman who lingered behind."

Let's fast forward to our 21st Century lifestyle using the Genesis story. Why did Mrs. Lot look back? Here it is, she was allowed to escape. She was being guided to safety by angels so why would she look back? The answer lies within all of us. It is in our unwillingness to let go. It is in our reluctance to let go of fear, anger, pain, the people, or events that are unhealthy for us: our energy-drainers. It is our lack of faith that prevents our future to be even brighter than our past.

We hold on to physical stuff as well - in the attic, basement, garage, shed, and closets. In many instances, we have long forgotten what the stuff is. Unfortunately, that is not the case with the mental storage that holds our hurt and resentment from two days ago, or was it 30 years ago? We hold on to relationships that died a year ago, or maybe 60 years ago. We hold on to toxic beliefs and situations and each time we look back on them a bit of us become a pillar of salt. We feel the dis-ease physically, mentally, emotionally maybe even financially. Like the time when I experienced back-to-back betrayals and pined for so long over - how could they? - that I contributed to my own financial meltdown.

In A New Earth, Author Eckhart Tolle teaches us about "the pain-body." Psychologists and Eastern Healers have made the connection between our emotional hurts and, whether immediately or over time, their potential to transform into physical bodily pain. Some of us will say, "Of course! You may remember the story of your grandfather being lynched." Maybe it is the memory of a tribal war and you are the only one to survive the massacre because you were covered by your mother's dead body. Or maybe it is being haunted by the gang-rape you endured as a child; being bullied or not being loved unconditionally.

Whatever it is that was stored in the attic of our memory has now seeped into our bodies, our lives, the way we relate with ourselves as well as with each other and it is causing us pain. This is why it is critical for us to have the desire to heal. These horrendous experiences may never be cured. However, the good news is, we can be healed – we do not have to look back, we can affirm that there is healing ahead. But first, we must have the desire to be healed. Whether we are in the care of mental health professionals or spiritual guides, healing starts with us being willing to create a healthy future.

Let us welcome each moment with its potential to heal. Take this time to notice your breathing – the inhalation and the exhalation. See how the body does it naturally? In comes the oxygen we need; out goes the carbon dioxide we do not need. Inhale. Exhale. Try this, as you inhale, create the vision in your mind of the future you desire. Exhale and forgive the past. Our co-healers (spiritual and professional) are waiting to take us to safety.

May we be guided to safety.

Yes! I Am willing to let go.

Self-Love

I Am My Beloved

I must confess. For the greater portion of my life, I struggled with the concept of self-love because I would equate self-love with selfishness. Any indication, any thought of showing love to myself would be instantly reversed, stopped, extinguished, vetoed, you name it, all in my effort to defeat being selfish. This behavior was informed by my childish understanding that my faith demanded that I love or take care of others, especially those less fortunate. I didn't learn about caring for and loving myself. Then, years later, I was reintroduced to Jesus' explanation of the greatest commandment.

You shall love the Lord your God with all your heart, and with all your soul, and with all your mind. This is the great and first commandment. And a second is like it. You shall love your neighbor as you love yourself. (Matthew 22:37-39)

Right there at the end "You shall love your neighbor as you love yourself" was my epiphany! Loving myself was not only acceptable but necessary. This discovery was validated when I later read that centuries ago, theologian and philosopher, Saint Thomas Aquinas had declared that "well-ordered self-love is right and natural."

I now know self-love to be one of the behaviors that undergirds successful existence, well, at least mentally. Living the belief is still a struggle. I still tangle the ideas of selfishness and self-love.

I thought I would use this commandment as part of a Valentine's Day presentation on Love. I thought of incorporating the three types of Love with which I was familiar– Eros, Philia, and Agape. To remind myself of these three I did some research. My curiosity was heightened, and I plunged deeper, excavating other forms of Love. Here are eight types of Love the ancient Greeks are credited to have identified:

1. Eros- sexual passion and desire; erotic Love: physical body
2. Philia- affectionate/platonic Love or friendship: mind
3. Storge- familial Love, kinship and familiarity, patriotism: memories
4. Ludus- playful Love, flirting, teasing: emotions
5. Mania or obsessive Love – a type of madness when there is imbalance between Eros and Ludus, extreme jealousy, dependency: survival instinct
6. Pragma or enduring Love – aged, matured, in harmony that has been formed over time showing patience, tolerance: unconscious
7. Philautia or Self Love – the healthiest form of Love caring for Self: soul
8. Agape or Selfless Love – Highest type of Love, boundless compassion, unconditional infinite empathy, love of nature, God, the stranger: Spirit

There it was listed, with its own name: Philautia and was described as the healthiest form of love – love for our Self which harmonizes with our soul, Self-Love! It is placed just one notch away from the highest form of Love – Agape which is associated with our Divinity or Spirit.

Like the commandment, Philautia says we can only love another if we truly love ourselves. We can only show compassion to others if we show compassion to ourselves. What is also true is that it is only when the light of self-love is turned on that love in any of its other forms becomes activated.

The physical body does not need love to be aroused. Sister Tina Turner was right when she sang, "What's love got to do with it?" Going through the list, the answer seems to be not much. It appears that friendships, memories, emotions, basic instincts all seem to exist from a primordial impulse and help to ground our being. Philautia and Agape, on the other hand, accept the anchoring of our somebodyness by the other forms of love but then ask us to look outside of our Selves to see that what is true for us is also true for our Other. Allowing us to attain Unconditional Love. But before Unconditional Love, we must visit the station where we love ourselves, where we accept ourselves, live in authenticity with our truth, the place where all aspects of our lives are harmonized, and our souls celebrate in peace.

It's more than an understanding for me now – this Self-Love. I am a believer. Yet there are those times when I look at my options and I choose the one that does not reflect Self-Love. In those times, I check in with the other places where I store love – memories, my body, mind, instinct, etc. and remember, get back up, turn around and decide to return to the presence of Self-Love. In African wisdom it is called Sankofa, looking back to retrieve the wisdom that is necessary to move forward. I do so because it is truly an essential ingredient in the foundation of building an enriched life.

May we be strengthened to practice Self-Love.

Yes! I Am loving Self-Love.

"If you truly love yourself,
you could never hurt another."

- The Buddha

I Am Aware

One Minute on A Saturday Morning

The sun is shining on those of us who are happy
as well as those of us who mourn.
The clouds drift east to west.

The dragonflies chase each other
just as the butterflies to their right do a
catch-me-if-you-can dance.

A leaf falls from the mango tree
Having completed its life's work
Just missing the duck taking a morning nap.
The grass seems still but I know it's growing.

Someone's air conditioner is humming
Competing with the buzzing of another's power tool,
Both about to be muted by the whirring of
the approaching light aircraft

The breeze rustles the leaves of the avocado tree
The windchime sways but decides it wasn't driven to make a sound
So, it settled on the gentility of a dance.

And me, sitting, finding community with this lot.
Enjoying the heat of the sun and the coolness of the breeze.
Thinking of the duck and of the butterflies and the dragonflies
Did I mention the lizards flirting with no regard to my sensibilities?

Here we are,
This one minute on a Saturday morning
In this spot on this life-giving blue orb.

May my minutes be lived in pure consciousness.

Yes! I Am aware.

Interconnectedness Part 1

I Am Interconnected

Have you had the experience of contacting someone and the person says, "I just thought of you?" This mystical encounter isn't new or unusual. It is known in numerous forms. Famed Psychologist, Carl Jung, speaks of the "collective unconsciousness". Unitarian Universalists think of it as "the interdependent web of all existence".

Throughout the ages, civilizations have honored and taught this truth. Zoroastrians told us: "Do not do unto others whatever is injurious to you." The Buddhists say: "Treat not others in ways that you yourself would find hurtful." In Islam, the teaching is: "Not one of you truly believes until you wish for others what you wish for yourself." From Christianity we learn: "In everything do to others as you would have them do to you." Out of Africa, we have a word from the Bantu people: "Ubuntu." It teaches that because you are, I am.

*May I know the love in me because it is only
then that I can greet the love in you.
May we seek opportunities to embrace the truth of
our interconnectedness.*

Yes! I Am embracing my interconnectedness.

Togetherness

I Am not Alone

A friend shared the pain felt when a family member chose to withdraw from the family. As I reflected on the conversation, I realized I understood her pain as well as the family member's desire to withdraw -they were both hurting.

Many times, if we truly examine the source of our pain, we will find that the latest cause is just the tip of the iceberg. It is rarely the origin. Few of us are skilled at dealing with our emotional or psychological injuries at the time of the incident. As a result, we bury them. Yet they do reappear, usually during the times when we cannot, or just refuse to make the link to the previous harm.

The next time your soul is yanked, try speaking to someone you trust – a professional, a friend. There are times when we should not be alone. We should not suffer alone. The Easter story in the Christian tradition tells us Jesus took three of his disciples with him to the Garden of Gethsemane on the night when he was burdened by his impending arrest. From the Judaic teachings we learn that

Moses took his brother, Aaron, to help by holding up his arms. Moses and Jesus benefited from human support. We mere mortals can do the same.

May we know that we are not alone.
May we find the support that is there for us.

Yes! It is so, I Am not alone.

Trinity of Partners

I Am my Glorious Life

I am fascinated by the various forms of the Trinity. Isis, Osiris, and Horus (Egyptian spirituality); The Father, Son, and Holy Ghost; Joseph, Mary, and Jesus (Christianity), Brahman, Vishnu and Parva (Hindu) and Ahura Mazda, Mithra and Anahita (Zoroastrianism). For some, it is the trinity of logic, reason, and faith. These and other forms of the Trinity are useful to the practitioners and the faithful to help us have a better understanding of our theology and beliefs.

However, it is Solomon's conversation with his God from the Judaic tradition (1 Kings: 3) that I find particularly captivating. We learn that God asked Solomon to seek his heart's desires. Solomon asked God to give him knowledge, understanding, and wisdom.

Though this happened ages ago, I truly believe such a request is still relevant. We should be asking for this Trinity of gifts. It is through the acquisition of knowledge on any topic that we have a deeper understanding of that subject and as a result, we become wiser.

The story goes on to tell us that not only did God grant Solomon knowledge, understanding, and wisdom but having secured this Trinity, God also showered him with another Trinity – riches, glory, and long life. Think how much richer your life would be if you acquired the knowledge to better understand so that you act more wisely.

May the power of the Trinity lift us to a glorious life of knowledge, understanding, and wisdom.

Yes! I Am embracing my glorious life.

A Courageous Life

I Am Sharing my Skills

When I was a child I learned about the parable of the talents (Matthew 25). Jesus told the story of an employer having a meeting with three of his workers. He told them that he would be going away but before he left, he gave one employee five talents, the second he gave two talents, and the third he gave one talent. Then they said their goodbyes.

After some time, the employer returned. He called the three workers to another meeting – like an evaluation. According to the story recorded in the Christian Bible, the first employee reported that he took his five talents, nurtured them, and was able to double what he was given and now had 10 talents. (The Gospel of the Nazarenes reports that the person who received the five talents squandered his enormous wealth on unhealthy living and was punished for his wasteful and licentious living. In this story only the second employee showed productivity and increased his talents.) The second employee also reported that he had doubled his gift. The third employee returned the one talent he was given. His only effort was to bury the talent.

Many of us hear this story and walk away inspired to use what skills we have to produce more – whatever our more is thought to be. Unfortunately, so many of us are like the third person. We do not honor what is ours. We look at others thinking the grass is greener over there. Or we allow fear to grip us. We allow the consciousness of lack to rule our actions and as a result, we stunt our growth and achievements.

This makes sense because so many times we are told to be safe. Maybe we heard, "Don't rock the boat." We see others being ridiculed for being different – outliers. We hear of people being jailed, harmed, or even killed for being bold and brave.

But our world is at a crossroads. We need new and diverse ways to advance humanity. It could be that the time is now for you and your one talent. Imagine that.

May we be bold and courageous as we share our skills to build our heaven.

Yes! I Am stepping into my Wholeness by using my Skills.

Divine Self

I Am Divine

I have read and heard about the story of Jesus and the Tempter for years. I've even heard sermons on this story. However, as I read the story again, I was struck by a minute detail. It occurred to me that for each temptation, Jesus was complicit, and I got the sense he was playing an active role.

The story, as told by the Books of Matthew, Mark, and Luke in the Christian Bible, takes us to the beginning of Jesus' ministry. Jesus had just ended his forty-days-and-forty-nights (code term for a long time) fast. We would imagine that by then he was starving. First, the Tempter enticed Jesus by saying, "If you are who you say you are then make the stones into bread" – ah the irresistible food! But Jesus was cool. He told the Tempter there is more to life than food. Then we are told Jesus went with the Tempter to another place where he was shown a breathtaking view and was told he could have it if he only worshipped the Tempter. Again, Jesus rebuffed the offer. For the third test, Jesus went with the Tempter to the highest peak where he was told to jump and not worry about being injured because the angels would rescue him. At this point,

Jesus scolded the Tempter who accepted defeat and they parted company.

Jesus was tempted with food, wealth or material possessions, and personal safety. This is how I heard the story for many years.

Recently, I saw the story through another lens. Jesus wasn't sitting minding his own business when the Tempter approached to inveigle him to do something contrary to his nature. In each of the three instances, we are told Jesus was led or was taken which meant Jesus voluntarily went with the Tempter.

If we believe Jesus is a miracle worker then we must believe Jesus had the power not to go with the Tempter and end the testing before it could start. But that's not what happened, and, in each case, we were taught to believe in our Truth and not to act contrary to our true nature. This shows us the importance of understanding the person we really are, understanding our personhood, our somebodyness.

The other lesson is who we hang out with. I think of the 'show me your friends and I will tell you who you are' lectures from my elders. Here we have Jesus hanging out with the Tempter. They went to not one, not two but three locations. Jesus knew whose company he was keeping but he was also confident in himself, his convictions. Jesus understood his own strengths.

In life, we think of ourselves as superior or inferior to our others. We choose who we will ignore. We create divisions and choose not to relate with these Others. Yet in this story, we learn how Jesus boldly interacted with the Tempter and wisely acted out of his own truth instead of embracing the Tempter's ideas.

It is comforting to converse with like-minds but there are benefits to listening to other views. Like Jesus, we can use the opportunity to authenticate and better define our lives. It may be an opportunity for us to fine-tune our values. We could very well have the chance to choose who we truly are. It took Jesus three chances to stand and affirm what he knew to be true. We, mere mortals, may have to get more than three opportunities. But the truth is, with resolve and a basic understanding of who we are, we can get there.

May I accept all my interactions knowing that in each incident there is the possibility to know my divinity.

Yes! I Am divine.

Self-Harmony

I Am One with All There is

The Semitic creation story is about one human female and one human male living in total harmony, perfect oneness in a garden. However, the time came when their actions exposed them to the duality of good and evil. As a result of learning about this polarity, the humans were banished from the garden and the unity they had grown to know was disrupted. They were now thrown in a world of right and wrong, up and down – a world that was no longer united.

When we look in the mirror, we see the features of our physical Self. We compare and determine its perfection or its deficiencies. We call ourselves names based on these observations. Should we close our eyes and quiet our Selves, looking within at our feelings and our thoughts may reveal someone else. How about when we dig deeper into our very essence? Does this Self reflect the one in the mirror? If we pronounce these two Selves to be different then it may be time to synthesize our contrasting Selves in order to return to our harmonized genesis.

Sufi sage, Rumi, using the original nature image says: "Out beyond ideas of wrongdoing and rightdoing, there is a field. I'll meet you there." Let's open our Self to his teaching and give our Self permission to move beyond the dualities in which we trap our Self.

When we can move beyond the different Self in the mirror and the Self at our core we move to our true Self. We break the veil from the snare of a comparative world and move beyond the duality that appears as our life. There is no judgement. We see life as the breath. It is one to inhale and exhale. Called by different names, serving different purposes, yet one. When we get there, we join Rumi in the field of Oneness.

Exhale, knowing that you have returned to your Garden. Inhale and feast on your Garden.

May I continue my journey to my unified Self.

Yes! I Am one with all of me.

My Calling

I Am Asking What is My Duty

A news headline highlighted the story of a politician giving the reason he was introducing a bill that would, seemingly, bring undue burden and even harm to a significant segment of the population. He declared that God told him to do it.

My first instinct was to query his understanding of God. What God would command him to introduce laws that would harm others? My mind was then flooded with the idea of our individual calling. Our religious and spiritual teachings are replete with people who were called to serve: some answered, some questioned the mission, some were bold, some were scared, yet for the most part, they eventually answered. Like the politician, they attributed their tasks to their God.

For many of us, when we say we serve God, it is usually a task that we find uplifting, beneficial to humanity and our world. Something that pleases our soul. But what if we are given a task that we find unpleasant? What if the execution of our calling – that thing that keeps popping in our minds, that thing that has a hold on us, that thing that excites us, yet it makes us so uncomfortable and uneasy that we keep hitting the pause button?

One of the Hindu scriptures, The Bhagavad Gita tells the story of Arjuna and Lord Krishna. It is a most powerful and instructive discourse on embracing the task at hand – even when it is unnerving. There are a number of lessons in this epic story but let's just consider the beginning.

Arjuna's side of the family was heir to half of the kingdom. His relatives who owned the other half were not satisfied owning half, so they unlawfully gained possession of the entire kingdom. After mediation failed, the only remaining method to solve the impasse was war.

As a Hindu, Arjuna believed in non-violence. Going into battle was distressing and countered his belief. To compound his agony, he looked on the people who would be maimed and killed in the war. They were his teachers, relatives, and friends – on both sides of the conflict. Overtaken with compassion he argued with Lord Krishna and emphatically stated he could not carry out such atrocities. "I see no use of killing my kinsmen in battle...I desire neither victory, nor pleasure, nor kingdom." Lord Krishna was having none of that and told Arjuna if he did "...not fight this righteous war, then you will fail in your duty."

As their dialogue continued Lord Krishna's Allness was revealed to Arjuna, who was "filled with wonder". He then worshiped and revered his Lord, who later told Arjuna to get on with the task. The battle is purposed: what is to be, already has been. Arjuna was the chosen one and all that was left to be done was for him to enter battle.

Yikes! Sounds harsh, but it worked.

Arjuna surrendered himself to Lord Krishna and in turn, Lord Krishna supported Arjuna's task. Together, they entered the battle and emerged victorious – the pre-ordained outcome.

This is the story of a battle fought in India around 3,000 BCE. But 5,000 years later we are still struggling to perform what is ours to do. What it is we are called to do. Arjuna knew his task. He just found it troubling, maybe even distasteful.

Some of us do not yet know our calling and are meandering our way to the fertile deltas which will allow the revelation. Some of us have an inkling, a knowing, a feeling of what is calling us. But we fear disappointing or harming a special human – a teacher, parent just like Arjuna. So, like Arjuna, take the time, now, to connect with your Source, your Creator, your Lord – the genesis of your calling. Trust and show reverence.

Some of us are certain of our path. We know that what we are doing is ours to do. It is ours to create heaven here on earth. It is the task we must undertake that will allow us to end our suffering and attain joy.

We each have our duty or our responsibility. Something that is ours to do. That thing when done in true service to our being, our somebodyness and in communion with our God, we will not find it necessary to broadcast it because the eternal light will shine on it and its beneficiaries, including you, will be transformed. Remember all of us are called but only few of us have chosen to answer.

To paraphrase an ancient Hebrew proverb, you are as you think in your heart. Perhaps we are to search our heart instead of our mind to find or hear what is calling us, that which belongs to each of us. Once we find it, we then release the distractions that have kept us from focusing on the journey to accomplishing this task.

When it is found, do not be surprised if these words with a tune bubble up:

> *"This little light of mine, I'm gonna let it shine; Oh, this little light of mine I'm gonna let it shine; yes, this little light of mine I'm gonna let it shine; let it shine, let it shine, let it shine!"*

Go on – dance.

May we experience the revelation of the task that is ours to perform and may we show reverence in its performance.

Yes! I Am being called.

Linked-up Living

I Am Practicing My Golden Rule

The first verse of the first chapter of the first book in the Hebrew Holy Bible reads (for the most part)

> In the beginning God created the heavens and the earth. The Earth was without form, and void and darkness were upon the face of the deep; and the Spirit of God (wind) was moving over the face of the waters.

For many of us formlessness, emptiness, and darkness are things to be avoided. They are really no - things. Our media and many in the society use the word 'dark' when what they really mean is frightful, unsettling, undesired, terrifying, or spine-chilling. Well, no need for this to become a Thesaurus, but I do hope you understand. Some of us use dark to distinguish from light - something that is desirable.

According to the biblical story, there was a trinity in the beginning: Water, Spirit of God, and Nothingness. Some may interpret darkness, formlessness, and emptiness as disorder. I'm going with Nothingness. The story credits the union of this trinity for the genesis of our world. A spark occurred or maybe it was a bang, and we, as a planet, a giant ecosystem, were off and running.

Many things have happened along our way since that spark. Degeneration and regeneration continue to be part of our evolution. Ideas and beliefs continue to unite and divide us. One idea, however, seems to keep popping up over time, in several cultures and religions. The idea of how to better relate with each other. It is called the Golden Rule.

Sometime ago I found a poster created by Scarboro Missions, A Canadian Catholic Community of Priests and Lay People, memorializing thirteen of the most popular Golden Rules. I added two.*

Zoroastrianism:
Do not do unto others whatever is injurious to yourself.

Confucianism:
One word which sums up the basis of all good conduct... lovingkindness. Do not do to others what you do not want done to yourself.

Taoism:
Regard your neighbor's gain as your own gain, and your neighbor's loss as your own loss.

Native American Thought:
We are as much alive as we keep the earth alive.

African Spirituality*

Ubuntu (one translation: Because you are, I am; because I am, you are)

Hinduism:

This is the sum of duty: do not do to others what would cause pain if done to you.

Buddhism:

Treat not others in ways that you yourself would find hurtful.

Sikhism:

I am a stranger to no one; and no one is a stranger to me. Indeed, I am a friend to all.

Jainism:

One should treat all creatures in the world as one would like to be treated.

Judaism

What is hateful to you, do not do to your neighbor. This is the whole Torah; all the rest is commentary.

Christianity:

In everything, do to others as you would have them do to you; for this is the law and the prophets.

Islam:
Not one of you truly believes until you wish for others what you wish for yourself.

Baha'i Faith:
Lay not on any soul a load that you would not wish to be laid upon you, and desire not for anyone the things you would not desire for yourself.

Unitarian Universalism:
We affirm and promote respect for the interdependent web of all existence of which we are a part.

Mayan Spirituality:*
In Lak'ech – I am another yourself or I am you and you are me.

One creation story began with a trinity of elements. Above is a guide to how our created humanity can relate to each other based on a trinity of words – The Golden Rule.

May The Golden Rule of our tradition or liking, remind us of our shared existence, our linked humanity, our belongingness.

Yes! I Am because of our Oneness.

My Book, My Life

I Am Reading My Book of My Life

The Christian Holy Bible informs readers how to practice Christianity - even though technically Christianity is about the Lord Jesus' teachings, therefore, I believe the information should be derived from all the Gospels: Synoptic, Coptic, Mary, Truth, etc. But that musing will be explored another time. This musing is about Western Christianity – Catholic and Protestant New Testament Gospels and not Coptic or Eastern Orthodox.

The stories in the books of the Holy Bible are varied. There are gruesome killings, pain being inflicted on individuals, wars, stories that uplift, stories that are heartwarming, stories that teach forgiveness, love stories, and stories with steps to seek revenge. Whatever actions you may choose, this collection has it.

What is true though, is that these stories were told to a particular community at a particular time. Take any of the letters sent by the Apostle Paul. They were written to a particular community - the Corinthians or the Galatians or a person e.g., Timothy, to give instructions, counsel, encouragement, etc.

Over the centuries these personal, targeted writings became universal. So, we read Paul's letter to the Ephesians and some of us preach that wives must submit to their husbands (Ephesians 5:22). Some believe this is the word of God. The interpretation is that the Christian God only speaks through these words written in the Christian Bible.

Unfortunately, this rationale takes away the reader's agency, sense of what feels true, the truth that we are children of this God, just as the many ancient writers of sacred texts, and that we too have the ability or even the right to be contemplative and listen for instructions from God. The belief that we are free to commune with God directly is thought to be heresy. While it is accepted that we may find comfort from the words of the Holy Bible, the idea that we may also receive guidance and comfort through our own quiet meditative time with our Creator is admonished.

The rebel Martin Luther came to this realization in the 16th Century. He is credited for saying "God writes the Gospel, not in the Bible alone, but also on trees, and in flowers and clouds and stars." I say Yes! to this truth. Let us take it up a notch and say that God's Gospels (good news) are also written in us. It's the realization Julian of Norwich had when she declared "And after this I saw God in an instant, that is in my understanding, and in seeing this I saw that he is in everything."

The Gospel of our God with all the light, truth, wisdom, and fortification for our journey, are waiting to be discovered or, better, uncovered within our Self.

May we be courageous and open the book that is our life. Go on.

Yes! I Am reading the Book of my Life.

Life Lives On

I Am Supporting my Descendants

"Your children are not your children. They are the sons and daughters of Life's longing for itself." - Kahlil Gibran, Writer/Poet

Almost 2,000 years ago Jesus told a remarkable story of a son who asked his father for his inheritance so he could leave home to experience the world. Many parents, perhaps, identify with the father and the fears or reservations he must have had as he said farewell to his son. (Luke 15: 11-32)

But do we really raise our children to be replicas of our Selves, to live our lives through them, or do we encourage them as they choose to be their own person? Do we teach them to fly and soar? Or something else. It's easy when their own somebodyness mirrors the parents' views of who they should be, but what happens when our children choose a different path, especially an unknown one? They choose a leader, a spouse, or a lifestyle that we deem unworthy or even unhealthy?

We share our views with our children knowing that we can never know what the Spirit or their Creator that resides in them is guiding them to do. We live in our own truths. Whether we differ or find similarities with them, we remind ourselves that love bears all things. Love is patient. Love is kind.

Our children may return home as in the story Jesus told or they may not. Either way, we love because we know love does not end. It reveals itself everywhere in everyone. Let's open our awareness to the light beings – our children.

May our descendants lovingly live in their truth and may we hold them up to face their sun.

Yes! I Am holding my descendants as they live their truth.

Life United Part 2

I Am Old and New

In the Gospel according to Matthew 13: 52, Jesus told his disciples "... every scribe who has been trained for the kingdom of heaven is like a householder who brings out of his treasure what is new and what is old." In some traditions, brides are taught to wear something old and something new.

There are value and wisdom in oldness. Just as there should be gleeful anticipation for what is new. This binary relationship of old and new is golden.

We, however, are engulfed in the falsehood that only what is new is to be considered, accepted, respected, admired. So much so that we created words such as 'seenager' to give seniors a sense of their teen years. Sometimes we use the term 'being of certain age' instead to convince ourselves we are hip, relevant, that we fit in what society or our peers consider to be youthful.

Our Pagan sisters honor three stages of the female – the Maiden, the Mother, and the Crone. Each stage plays a role in her growth and at the appropriate time, she releases the former stage in anticipation of her advancement to the next stage of her beingness. To paraphrase Jesus, the Pagan female treasures what is old and what is new.

May we know that the new, as well as the old,
have value in our lives.
May we know when each is necessary for our growth.

Yes! I Am old and new.

Interconnectedness Part 2

We Are Connected

"I will do as I please – it is my life!" These words ended a short and contentious telephone conversation with his father. So many of us have either expressed that belief or had it said to us. But how true is it to say, "This is my life?"

It may appear to be true. French Philosopher Rene Descartes famously announced, "I think, therefore, I am." And yes, although we feel, we communicate, we eat, our parents cannot feel our heartbreaks and the pain of our disappointments. No one else experiences the mountain-top joys we live through. So, it is easy to believe that this is MY LIFE. We own it. We accept our responsibilities – they are ours and ours alone.

Yet that view is only true when we are in the midst of the forest of self. When we step away and see the panoramic view of our Selves, we see that we are connected to our parents and other family members. We see generations and generations. When we look at the people who taught us, provided our food, culture, housing, transportation, and all the amenities we rely on, we see a network that stretches outside of our home, community, and even our city. Now think about the people who are connected to these people. Then consider Mother Earth, the rain, the sun, the cosmos without which our life would not exist.

Buddhist Monk and Peace Activist, Thích Nhất Hạnh calls this our inter-being. The Celts name our twining-sanctified-connection "Anam Cara". By any name, we know the Truth. We are connected.

May we come to know we are not alone.
May we understand we are a part of the whole.

Yes! I Am a link in the sacred connection called life.

Connected Self

I Am Connected to Life

Many of us accept the details of Jesus' birth as recorded in the Gospels of Matthew and Luke. The same is true for those of us who believe in the Easter stories as stated in the Gospels. There are also many of us who are not sure whether these two stories are culturally or historically accurate. And, too, there are many who believe these stories are definitely not true.

Interestingly, even among those who believe the stories have been overstated or inaccurate, is the belief that Jesus was an historic figure. For example, Muslims revere Jesus but do not believe that he is the son of God. Jesus' adherents see him as a divine being worthy to be worshiped. Some see him as one of the coolest proponents of health care for everyone, him healing the sick without questioning their worthiness. Others see him in the role he described himself, a Way-Shower (John 14:6-12) - one who shows the way.

As the latter, he taught us how to live our lives in this physical world. He taught us how to turn over the tables when we see injustice, greed, and wrongdoing. He showed us how to care for each other. He told us not to judge each other. He demonstrated how we should remain connected with the Source of our being. He taught us how to have fun. We see him being sad and anxious. Very importantly, he taught us lessons in forgiveness and love.

I believe these lessons are wrapped up in his belief that we are to love each other in the manner we love ourselves. That the good we desire for ourselves is what we should desire for others because as he said: "I am in the Father and you in me and I in you (John 14:20)." This bonding, this unity enforces the central idea in Jesus' lesson that we are connected. We are one.

We should take away the lesson that we die when we separate ourselves from the whole. We become less of who we are. We have a sense of liveliness when we are connected. We become invigorated and sparks of life emanate from us.

May we open our hearts to what is true: our interconnectedness gives us life.

Yes! I Am connected to the web of life.

My Gifts

I Am Sharing My Gift

The Queen is dead! Long live the Queen!

I recall receiving one of the most enduring gifts – a gift of songs. It was 1973 when a friend loaned me Aretha Franklin's Amazing Grace album. I was never one to fidget with or even admire gadgets but after the first play, I could not stay away from the album and our new Grundig stereo console.

The hymns of my dear Brownsville Presbyterian church had not prepared me for such awakening. Yes, I know that so-called secular music could stir my soul and move my feet, but I was ignorant to the fact that music celebrating the Divine, church-music could stir me. It could make me feel like touching the sky, cause me to stop and listen and move my body. It could motivate me to re-read the story of Mary and Martha and Jesus. I read again how this woman put Jesus in his place: "If you had come when we called you, our brother would not have died!" Can you imagine the anger, the telling-off?

Years later, in another century Ms. Franklin showed up with her iconic hat and led us in celebrating U.S. President Barack Obama's inauguration. And yes, she sang. And again, she transported me to a place of Allness. I have never heard angels, but I've heard her. In those moments I am thrilled and in rapturous bliss.

She has now transitioned from this physical life. I remember 1973 when she came into my life. I am so much richer, and in fact, the world is enriched because she sang. She shared the treasure that is her voice.

Let us not just remember her voice, her songs. She shared what she had. Aretha shone her light and gave us joy, hope, and enrichment.

Let us be reminded that we too, have gifts and our task is to share them.

May we respect our gifts so that we can release them.

Yes! I Am Sharing my Gifts.

I Am Saying Yes to Me

Yes

Each time I see the rainbow
I say, Yes!
I look at the night sky
I see planets and stars
I see the North Star and
I wonder about Harriet, the Quakers, Underground Railroads
And I hear the freedom-seeking voices saying Yes!
I hear the drum and the bass and the sax
My body says Yes!
I see the blue of the sea
I didn't swim but I said, Yes!
To its power and beauty
I say Yes! to the sun's energy and
Yes! To the rain's freshness
Yes! To the display of colors by the bougainvillea
And Yes! To the lilac and gardenia's sweet fragrance
At times, I say Yes, but...

At times it's Yes, and...
Yes, resides in the silence
Yes, comforts the inner child
I walk closer to my mirror
Wanting to feel the truth
Yes! To who and all I am

"The greatest thing in the world is to know how to belong to oneself."

Michel de Montaigne,
The Complete Essays

Now, What?

I started writing Yes! I Am months before COVID-19, the novel coronavirus, became a pandemic, or dare I say, even thought of. Yet here it is in our midst. Impacting the lives of most of the over seven billion of us here on Earth. At the time of this writing, worldwide, over 110,000,000 people tested positive for the virus, over 85,000,000 recovered and over 2,500,000 persons have succumbed to the illnesses brought on by the virus.

The immediate changes are the loss of loved ones or care needed for survivors who have now developed long-term health issues. For those of us not directly impacted by COVID-19, the way of life we had may be permanently changed. Air travel, wearing masks, being more vigilant about personal hygiene, how we work, how we socialize and so many other aspects of living could be changed.

When COVID-19 was declared a pandemic by the World Health Organization, many countries closed their borders. Governments instituted shelter-in-place policies. People lost their source of income or were forced to work from home. The introverts among us thought they were in heaven. They could now stay in the comfort of their homes. They were no longer forced to mingle and engage in polite conversations. However, for others this was torturous.

We can choose any of the myriad of reasons that caused us discomfort. Maybe we had a small apartment. Maybe it is a tiny apartment without access to outdoor space. It could be we needed the stimulation from others. It could be that we are forced to spend time with ourselves, something we have spent a lifetime running from.

For many of us, the modern-technological-enhanced lifestyle has so many options to lead us away from paying attention to our Selves. The array of competing distractions can, instead, provide sensory satisfaction.

Then COVID-19 arrived and quietened our busy-ness. Scientists reported that pollution was reduced, the Earth's upper crust shook less, which resulted in a drop in seismic noise. Many of us listened to Mother Earth and stilled ourselves, accepting this as a time to re-set our vibrations and rid ourselves of harmful practices. We took the time to go within to re-member the human we were created to be.

It was in this silencing when the world exploded. The silence allowed many to see injustice and brutality. To remember how they experienced or knew of generational hurts that were instituted and practiced to demean, take away a people's dignity and humanity.

In small villages and large cities, throughout the world, people allied with the African-American-originated Black Lives Matter movement and marched to unmask the brutality and injustices that have harmed and traumatized their own communities.

The mystics we learn from, ancient or modern, place a high value on contemplative practices – meditation, labyrinth walking, praying, walking, and others. The late U.S. Congressman and Civil Rights icon, John Lewis, called protesting for justice and equality, Good Trouble. Perhaps we can add Good Trouble to this list.

It seems this intersectional existence of silence and raising our voices is a perfect stepping off point to live in our oneness believing as the Mayans, "I am another yourself". Thomas Merton, Trappist monk, shared that it is in the deep solitude that he found the gentleness with which he could truly love his brother and sister. Perhaps the silencing forced on us by COVID-19 is an opportunity for us to witness injustice and open us up to the truth that we, those administering or benefiting from injustice as well as those who feel the burden of being pinned down, deserve better. We see that we are linked in this combat that harms all of us. Perhaps the time gave us voice and we are inspired to heed the wisdom of the mystic Rumi, "Don't go back to sleep."

My wish is that you, dear Reader, take advantage of this genesis, whether in the silence or the protest and know that you deserve to be free to be all you were created to be, to be loved unconditionally, to share your skills, to love deeply and immensely, especially your own Self. This time is pregnant with possibilities, and it is waiting for your declaration of life, *Yes! I Am.*

"A House divided within it Self cannot stand.
I will, therefore, nourish and integrate my Body, Mind, Soul, and
Spirit - the physical, mental, emotional and spiritual - that have
combined to manifest as me."

*I Am Precious: Nourishing Nuggets for the Heart;
Genuine Gems for the Soul*

ABOUT THE AUTHOR

Opal Murray is an ordained Interfaith Minister and has served as a: retreat facilitator, probation officer, banker, systems analyst, information management coordinator, transportation coordinator, community organizer, grant writer, program manager, executive director, volunteer manager, and training coordinator. She is also a Veteran of the U.S. Army.

She's graduated magna cum laude from Spelman College where she was presented with the Shirley Chisholm Award for Leadership. She holds a Master of Public Administration degree from Troy State University and was ordained by One Spirit Interfaith Seminary.

A spiritual health advocate, she has found inspiration in the interfaith, interconnected stories of hope, love, compassion, resilience, faith, courage, fortitude, forgiveness, purpose, and cooperation.

She currently resides in Florida.

Connect with the author at www.livingouroneness.com

www.ingramcontent.com/pod-product-compliance
Lightning Source LLC
Chambersburg PA
CBHW062008040426
42447CB00010B/1973